humble and holy

DEVOTIONS FOR ADVENT & CHRISTMAS 2025–2026

AUGSBURG FORTRESS

Minneapolis

HUMBLE AND HOLY

Devotions for Advent & Christmas 2025–2026

Copyright © 2025 Augsburg Fortress. All rights reserved. Except for brief quotations in critical articles or reviews, no part of this book may be reproduced in any manner without prior written permission from the publisher. Visit www.augsburgfortress.org/info/permissions or write to Permissions, Augsburg Fortress, Box 1209, Minneapolis, MN 55440.

References to ELW are from *Evangelical Lutheran Worship*, copyright © 2006 Evangelical Lutheran Church in America. References to ACS are from *All Creation Sings*, copyright © 2020 Augsburg Fortress.

Scripture quotations are from the *New Revised Standard Version Updated Edition*, copyright © 2021 National Council of the Churches of Christ in the United States of America. Used by permission. All rights reserved worldwide.

"Household blessings and prayers" are from *Bread for the Day 2025: Daily Bible Readings and Prayers*, copyright © 2024 Augsburg Fortress.

ISBN 979-8-8898-3727-5
eISBN 979-8-8898-3729-9

Writers: Lydia Posselt (November 30–December 6), Michael Girlinghouse (December 7–13), Harvard Stephens Jr. (December 14–21), Lisa A. Smith (December 22–27), Michael Coffey (December 28–January 1), Angela T. !Khabeb (January 2–6)

Editor: Laurie J. Hanson
Cover design: Alisha Lofgren
Cover and interior images: All images © Getty Images. Used by permission.
Interior design and typesetting: Eileen Engebretson

The paper used in this publication meets the minimum requirements of American National Standard for Information Sciences—Permanence of Paper for Printed Library Materials, ANSI Z329.48-1984

Printed in China.

25   1 2 3 4 5

Welcome

Humble and Holy continues a centuries-old Christian tradition of setting aside time to prepare for the celebration of Jesus' birth and to anticipate his return. The Advent season of preparation then unfolds in the joy of the twelve days of Christmas and the day of Epiphany.

This devotional offers daily devotions for the first Sunday of Advent (November 30, 2025) through Epiphany (January 6, 2026). These devotions explore the humble and the holy in year A scripture readings (in the Revised Common Lectionary) for the Sundays of Advent and Christmas, as well as for the festival days and commemorations in the Advent and Christmas seasons. The writers bring their unique voices and pastoral wisdom to these texts, and offer the voices of other witnesses in the quotations they have chosen for the "To ponder" sections. The devotional also provides household blessings and prayers (see pages 81–93) to enrich your preparations and celebrations during the Advent and Christmas seasons.

May the humble and holy birth of the Christ child bring you joy, love, and peace throughout the year!

November 30 / Advent 1

Isaiah 2:1-2
The word that Isaiah son of Amoz saw concerning Judah and Jerusalem.
In days to come
the mountain of the Lord's house
shall be established as the highest of the mountains
and shall be raised above the hills;
all the nations shall stream to it.

To ponder
Having faith . . . addresses intimidating circumstances with defiant confidence in God.—Gabby Cudjoe-Wilkes and Andrew Wilkes, *Psalms for Black Lives*

Waiting with confidence in God

Welcome to Advent! I love this season, but I find myself stressed this time of year. Maybe you feel that way today too. We can get derailed very quickly on the Advent journey. We want to reflect with holy anticipation and quiet excitement on the coming birth of Jesus. At the same time, this might be the busiest time of the year, with decorating, gift-giving, attending worship services and special events, and celebrating with friends and family. All these things can add to the everyday stresses of balancing work and relationships and just trying to make ends meet.

This Advent season may not go the way we hope or plan. We may not be as reflective or excited or energetic as we would like to be. Our plans might change due to weather conditions, illness, or financial challenges. But as we wait, know that God is with us, sometimes in surprising and unexpected ways, and God's word still arrives as a message of love as tall as any mountain and as steady as any stream.

Prayer

Even when we trip over our good intentions, O God, guide our days this Advent season. Give us confidence and hope in this time of waiting, and empower us to carry your message of love to all the world. Amen.

December 1

Isaiah 2:3
Many peoples shall come and say,
"Come, let us go up to the mountain of the Lord,
to the house of the God of Jacob,
that he may teach us his ways
and that we may walk in his paths."

To ponder
Jesus didn't come to make things marginally more bearable.
—Austen Hartke, *Transforming*

Going up the Advent mountain

The fallen leaves crunch underfoot, brittle and disintegrating into dust. The gorgeous fall foliage is just a memory. The briskness of October and November has given way to a bite in the air, turning your breath into vapor. This is only the start of the Advent path, but already it inclines sharply upward. The smooth entrance was soothing until the first rock poked through the path, then another, then another. The sign you passed clearly pointed in this direction . . . or did it? Is this the right way? The path curves ahead, so there is no way to know for sure—except to keep going.

You hear crunching leaves from behind and wonder—Is this friend or foe? A smiling face comes alongside you and says, "Come, let's go up this mountain together! You are not alone; I'll go with you." You and your companion walk together toward the summit. On the way, God's peace and presence is with you and all others taking this path.

Prayer

Jesus my Lord and leader at my side, please guide, encourage, and strengthen my flagging steps, and help me to accompany others along the way. Amen.

December 2

Isaiah 2:3-4
For out of Zion shall go forth instruction
and the word of the LORD from Jerusalem.
He shall judge between the nations
and shall arbitrate for many peoples.

To ponder
Follow the love. That will never lead you wrong.—Cindy Maddox, *In the Neighborhood of Normal*

Guide to the best Advent
Wouldn't it be awesome if Advent came with an instruction manual? While many Christians around the world are observing the season of Advent, others have been in full-blown

Christmas mode for weeks now. Some voices try to tell us how to give the perfect gifts and have the best Christmas ever, but following their instructions can take us down a path that ends in credit card debt, strained relationships, a planet in peril, and widespread anxiety.

Another voice, echoing Isaiah's words, reminds us that another way is not only possible, but vital. This is the way of love. We need one another. We need to help and encourage each other to follow the "instructions" and the way of Jesus. Step one: Love God. Step two: Love all people. Step three: Love yourself. Step four: Follow the Love.

Prayer

Holy God, we need you and we need one another on this Advent journey. Focus our hearts and minds on your voice and your teaching. Be with us as we follow your love, wherever you may take us. Amen.

December 3

Isaiah 2:4-5
They shall beat their swords into plowshares
and their spears into pruning hooks;
nation shall not lift up sword against nation;
neither shall they learn war any more.
O house of Jacob,
come, let us walk
in the light of the Lord!

To ponder
In fighting for what we consider to be right, we can too easily lose sight of what is good.—Dorcas Cheng-Tozun, *Social Justice for the Sensitive Soul*

Do you hear God's song?

Several years ago, a film adaptation of *Les Misérables* was released to great acclaim. This musical tells the intertwining stories of a reformed convict on the run, his adopted child growing up, and the residents of Paris tragically caught up in the latest revolution. As I watched the final scene of the movie, I noticed props that seemed out of place. Nearly the entire cast held weapons of war as they sang about peace to a swelling orchestral score. Had the producers taken the time to listen to the lyrics? Hadn't they watched the rest of the movie?

All too often in our lives, we hear the words God is singing into our hearts, but don't really listen. We take up instruments of death and uphold systems that harm, while claiming to be on the side of life. All the while, God is breaking our weapons, breaking down barriers, and transforming violence and death into life.

Prayer

Lord, lead us in your radical way of peace. Banish our desire to hide or to fight. Instead, embolden us with love for our neighbors throughout the world. Amen.

December 4

Matthew 24:32-35

[Jesus said,] "From the fig tree learn its lesson: as soon as its branch becomes tender and puts forth its leaves, you know that summer is near. So also, when you see all these things, you know that [the Son of Man] is near, at the very gates. Truly I tell you, this generation will not pass away until all these things have taken place. Heaven and earth will pass away, but my words will not pass away."

To ponder

It is not weakness . . . that we are captivated by stories. We were meant to be drawn into the true divine drama.—Kaitlyn Schiess, *The Ballot and the Bible*

Once upon an ending

In this gospel reading from Matthew for the First Sunday in Advent, Jesus and his disciples are in Jerusalem for Passover. Peter, John, and the rest of them are doing the typical touristy things. I can imagine the disciples gawking over the Temple Mount, as we do when we drive past a home that is beautifully lit for Christmas. Jesus, however, knows something that the disciples don't: he has only a few days to live. Instead of admiring the buildings, Jesus discusses their future destruction. He had already mentioned wars and suffering, trials and false messiahs earlier in Matthew's gospel. All of this left the early followers of Jesus wondering: Can God still show up even when everything looks so bleak?

God does show up in Jesus—Jesus who came, who comes, and who will come again. Jesus came into a world that looked bleak for all but a powerful few. He comes to us today in baptismal water and the word, in bread and wine, and through scripture. Jesus will come again to bring in his reign of love. We watch for signs of Jesus coming again, even as he and his reign are already at work here among us.

Prayer

God of the thin places, of the in-between, of all times and locations, thank you for the gift of your Son, today, tomorrow, and forever. Amen.

December 5

Matthew 24:36-39

[Jesus continued,] "But about that day and hour no one knows, neither the angels of heaven, nor the Son, but only the Father. For as the days of Noah were, so will be the coming of the Son of Man. For as in the days before the flood they were eating and drinking, marrying and giving in marriage, until the day Noah entered the ark, and they knew nothing until the flood came and swept them all away, so, too, will be the coming of the Son of Man."

To ponder

I think there's something beautiful about being lucky enough to witness a thing on its way out.—Becky Chambers, *A Psalm for the Wild-Built*

And something new is being born

Noah's ark is a beloved story in children's nurseries and storybooks. What can go wrong with cute animals and a boat? The truth is that behind the cuteness there is the death and destruction of all but Noah and his family before the story ends with the rainbow sign of a promise. Similarly, in our beloved nativity sets and pageants, we have cute, quiet animals, clean hay, and vibrant costumes, but nothing at the birth of Jesus would have been very clean or completely silent!

During Advent a new thing is being born in us. This is messy, but that is exactly where Jesus inserts himself. We don't know when or how, but Jesus is on his way. It's difficult for us to be patient when the world around us wants to skip ahead to a happy ending or get what we want or need right away. But here is good news: We wait for something we indeed already have—Jesus is in our midst now.

Prayer

Transformational God, birth in us your ways of love for a world in need. Amen.

December 6

Matthew 24:42-44

[Jesus said,] "Keep awake, therefore, for you do not know on what day your Lord is coming. But understand this: if the owner of the house had known in what part of the night the thief was coming, he would have stayed awake and would not have let his house be broken into. Therefore you also must be ready, for the Son of Man is coming at an hour you do not expect."

To ponder

I believe we also light [Advent candles] as symbols of a world we imagine to be possible when Jesus comes to earth—a world where hope, peace, joy, and love will reign.—Callie E. Swanlund, *From Weary to Wholehearted*

Advent scavenger hunt

Each December for a few years, church youth groups from Mercer County, New Jersey, descended on the local mall, with its Santas, tinsel, and bright blinking lights—not to shop for gifts but to recreate and take photos of Advent signs. Memorable moments included a youth dressed as a faux-fur-wearing John the Baptist, and another carefully swaddled in coats and hats to look something like baby Jesus.

You too can find signs of Advent in this holiday-saturated December—and not just at a mall or in a church. The words *hope*, *peace*, *joy*, or *love* might remind you of the names some use for the candles in an Advent wreath. Drinking a cup of coffee could encourage you to "keep awake" while waiting for Jesus' arrival. Adding an event to your calendar could help you to remember that we don't know the day or time when Jesus will return. There are endless possibilities. Looking for Advent signs can prepare us to see where Jesus is breaking into and interrupting our lives at this busy and hectic time of year. Keep awake!

Prayer

Dear Jesus, we are often impatient. Help us to stay in the moment as we prepare and wait for your arrival. Amen.

December 7 / Advent 2

Isaiah 11:1-3
A shoot shall come out from the stump of Jesse,
and a branch shall grow out of his roots.
The spirit of the Lord shall rest on him,
the spirit of wisdom and understanding,
the spirit of counsel and might,
the spirit of knowledge and the fear of the Lord.
His delight shall be in the fear of the Lord.

To ponder
Knowing trees, I understand the meaning of patience.
Knowing grass, I can appreciate persistence.—Hal Borland,
Countryman

The patience of paper farmers

I grew up in a paper mill town. All around the town, tall thin pine trees grew in straight lines. It took twenty-five years for those trees to grow to maturity. When the trees were ready for harvest, they were clear-cut and taken away, leaving large open spaces in the forest. New trees were planted, but it was a few years before their little green heads could be seen poking up through the foliage, the promise of a harvest many years away. Paper farmers are very patient people!

Speaking of patience, it was approximately seven hundred years between Isaiah's time and the birth of Jesus. It has been around two thousand years since a shoot from the stump of Jesse became a branch and that branch became a tree, and a long time since Jesus sent his apostles into the world to continue his ministry. Today, Jesus' mission of love, grace, and new life continues to grow toward the future harvest.

During this season of watching and waiting, we can see new green branches poking their heads up all around us. With the patience of a paper farmer, those signs of hope can sustain us even as we look to the day when Jesus comes, not to cut us down, but to raise us up into the fullness of God's reign.

Prayer

Jesus, grant us patience and courage as we wait and watch for your coming, even as we live now in the promise and hope of God's reign. Amen.

December 8

Isaiah 11:3-4
He shall not judge by what his eyes see
or decide by what his ears hear,
but with righteousness he shall judge for the poor
and decide with equity for the oppressed of the earth.

To ponder
He rules the world with truth and grace
and makes the nations prove
the glories of his righteousness
and wonders of his love, and wonders of his love,
and wonders, wonders of his love.
—"Joy to the world," ELW 267

Through holy eyes

Through wide, wonder-filled eyes the child in us looks at the sparkling lights and decorations that surround us during this time of year. The sounds and songs of the season can be heard in stores, homes, and churches, setting the tone for shopping, gatherings, and worship. Ideally, Christmas movies and shows reflect themes of joy, generosity, and goodwill.

But there is a different side to this time of year too, isn't there? Wars continue to rage among nations. Many people don't have access to adequate food, housing, or health care. Others are weighed down by loneliness and grief. In these and many more ways, the peace on earth that we yearn for isn't reflected in the world around us.

God sees those who are poor, hears the cries of those who are oppressed, and acts to alleviate their suffering. As people of faith, we are called to do the same, bringing peace and joy to the world.

Prayer

God of truth and grace, open our hearts and minds to reach out to those for whom life is difficult. Help us to share the wonders of your love. In Jesus' holy name, amen.

December 9

Isaiah 11:6-8
The wolf shall live with the lamb;
the leopard shall lie down with the kid;
the calf and the lion will feed together,
and a little child shall lead them.
The cow and the bear shall graze,
their young shall lie down together;
and the lion shall eat straw like the ox.
The nursing child shall play over the hole of the asp,
and the weaned child shall put its hand on the adder's den.

To ponder
In God's "kin-dom" non-traditional relationships are given pride of place, for they are often more authentic because they are not in thrall to patterns of domination.—Thomas Bohache, in *The Queer Bible Commentary*

Predators and prey
The little girl, not more than six or seven, stood on the front step of the house holding a bucket up to her mother. Mom took a step back when she saw what was in the bucket—snakes, half a dozen of them! "Wh . . . Where did you get those?" Mom said. "I saved them from the woodpile," the little girl replied with a proud smile. "Can we keep them in the house? It's getting cold." Mom put a hand on her daughter's shoulder and said, "Snakes live in the woodpile. We should take them back to their home." As they walked back to the woodpile, Mom explained that not all snakes are friendly.

Isaiah's vision of God's reign includes unlikely, harmonious relationships between predators and prey: wolves and lambs, bears and cows, snakes and children. It's a reign of peace, even between mortal enemies. Jesus, the Prince of peace, gathers up people in his bucket—even those you might not expect—saving us all with childlike grace and love.

Prayer
Lord Jesus, move us and your church to embrace all people with humility and love, knowing you first embraced us. Amen.

December 10

Isaiah 11:9
They will not hurt or destroy
on all my holy mountain,
for the earth will be full of the knowledge of the Lord
as the waters cover the sea.

To ponder
Only a dwelling place of the breadth and depth of God can finally count and hold all the days, weeks and years of humankind.—Dorothy C. Bass, *Receiving the Day*

Small wonders
My wife and I like to sit on our patio and watch the sun set over the Black Mountains of Arizona. They are aptly named,

because, as the sun settles behind them, they become massive black silhouettes against the glowing sky. As the sky darkens, the stars slowly emerge, and the sparkling night sky dwarfs the mountains. Watching this nightly show makes one feel small with wonder.

I imagine the prophet had a similar humbling vision as he considered the vastness of the sea and contemplated the day when the shoot of Jesse would bring peace to a world terrified by the approaching Assyrian armies. This would be a time when God's steadfast love and the people's faithfulness would put an end to suffering and violence.

During this Advent time we also look forward to the day when God's reign comes in all its fullness, bringing justice, wholeness, and everlasting peace to all creation—the reign of God promised in the newborn babe in the manger and revealed in Jesus' life, death, and resurrection; the new life offered to us through the waters of baptism, and the vastness of the promise those waters contain; the humbling vision of the God who created the mountains, and the stars loving us enough to come and walk among us.

Prayer

Holy one, you created the vastness of the sea and the wonders of the heavens. Create in us an awareness of the vastness of your love and the wonder of your advent. Amen.

December 11

Matthew 3:1-3

In those days John the Baptist appeared in the wilderness of Judea, proclaiming, "Repent, for the kingdom of heaven has come near." This is the one of whom the prophet Isaiah spoke when he said,
"The voice of one crying out in the wilderness:
'Prepare the way of the Lord; make his paths straight.'"

To ponder

Church, somewhere along the way, we started to believe what the world was saying about us.—Lenny Duncan, *Dear Church*

Preparing the way

More than forty years ago, I heard a pastor preach about John the Baptist raising up valleys and lowering mountains to prepare the way of the Lord. The pastor went on to say that all ministry should reflect John's by preparing the way for people to hear the good news of Jesus Christ. This means breaking down the barriers and filling in the pitfalls that too often trip people up or get in the way of hearing and responding to the gospel message.

Today there are all sorts of things that prevent people from receiving the gospel. The culture around us has prevented this by providing countless distractions and ways to fill our time, and by reinforcing the notion that we can live life without God. And instead of continually smoothing the path, the church also has held back the gospel by building barriers of exclusion, marginalizing people, and digging pitfalls by keeping things the way they always have been.

God's reign is breaking into our world, into our lives, and into the lives of people outside church walls—sometimes where we least expect it. John's cry to prepare the way of the Lord—wherever it leads us—continues today.

Prayer

Empower us with your Spirit, O Lord, to break down barriers, fill in pitfalls, and straighten paths so everyone receives the good news that the Christ child is God's gift of love to all. Amen.

December 12

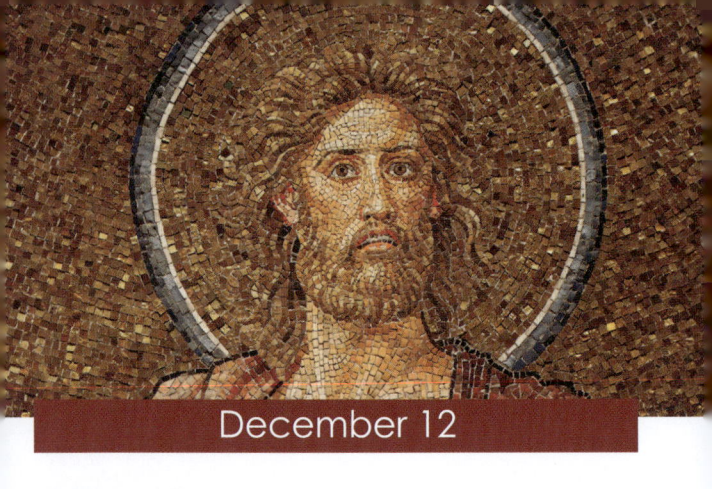

Matthew 3:4-6
Now John wore clothing of camel's hair with a leather belt around his waist, and his food was locusts and wild honey. Then Jerusalem and all Judea and all the region around the Jordan were going out to him, and they were baptized by him in the River Jordan, confessing their sins.

To ponder
We are beggars, this is true.—Martin Luther

Humble, holy faith
She lived in her car and scraped together a living as best she could by performing for passersby. I knew her story, how she had wound up on her corner. But she was more than the

misfortunes she had suffered along the way. She was a child of God. Although she had been broken down by life, she trusted wholly in God. The witness of her humble, holy faith moved me, taught me, inspired me.

John the Baptist's ascetic appearance was like the prophet Elijah's (2 Kings 1:8). His diet was very simple. He lived in the wilderness, the place where the Israelites had once lived, protected by God. From that place John called people—rich and poor, powerful and powerless—to repentance. He washed the people in the flowing waters of the Jordan to prepare them for the One who was coming, the one born among us so we might know that we too are children of God.

Martin Luther's last words were reported to be "We are beggars, this is true." Before God, we are all broken-down, impoverished people, scraping along as best we can. But through the work of the Spirit, we repent and turn to God, learn to trust in God, and live as God's children.

Prayer

Merciful God, we need you. We need your grace, your mercy, your forgiveness. Through your Spirit, turn our hearts to you, wash us clean, and remind us again that we are all your children through Jesus Christ our Lord. Amen.

December 13

Matthew 3:11
[John said,] "I baptize you with water for repentance, but the one who is coming after me is more powerful than I, and I am not worthy to carry his sandals. He will baptize you with the Holy Spirit and fire."

To ponder
Many of our prairies and forests actually need fire to remain healthy and thrive.—Jennifer Fawcett, "Ask an Expert: Why Is Prescribed Fire Important?"

Prescribed burns

Not long after I began working in Arizona, the air around the ministry center was filled with smoke. I knew Arizona could have devastating forest fires. I went outside and saw smoke billowing up beyond the mountains to the west. My adrenaline shot up and I was ready to run! Curiously, no one else seemed concerned. I asked the office manager about it. "Nothing to worry about," they said. "It's a prescribed burn." (That's a controlled fire used to prevent catastrophic wildfires and maintain ecosystems.)

While the fire of the Holy Spirit is anything but controlled by human means, it is a burn prescribed by God that "has called [us] through the gospel, enlightened [us] . . . , made [us] holy and kept [us] in the true faith." In the same way the Spirit "calls, gathers, enlightens, and makes holy the whole Christian Church . . . and keeps it with Jesus Christ in the one common, true faith" (Luther's Small Catechism). This Pentecost fire fills us, motivates us, and sends us out in mission and ministry to do the "good works, which God prepared beforehand so we may walk in them" (Ephesians 2:10), wherever that uncontrollable Holy Fire may take us.

Prayer

Spirit of the Living God, wash over us as we prepare to celebrate Jesus' birth and step into the future God is, even now, preparing for us. Burn in our hearts and lives so that we might bring the light and life of Christ wherever we go. Amen.

December 14 / Advent 3

Isaiah 35:1-2, 4, 6-7
The wilderness and the dry land shall be glad;
the desert shall rejoice and blossom;
like the crocus it shall blossom abundantly
and rejoice with joy and shouting.
The glory of Lebanon shall be given to it,
the majesty of Carmel and Sharon.
They shall see the glory of the Lord,
the majesty of our God. . . .
Say to those who are of a fearful heart,
"Be strong, do not fear!
Here is your God." . . .
For waters shall break forth in the wilderness
and streams in the desert;

the burning sand shall become a pool
and the thirsty ground springs of water.

To ponder

It occurred to me that as much as I think I am waiting on God, as much as I struggle with this between time of my prayer and God's answer, perhaps God is also waiting on me.—Yolanda Pierce, "The Spirituality of Waiting"

I am with you always

God calls us to take heart and to encourage other people. A fearful heart can be full of doubt and anxiety, but God keeps sending us into the world with the good news of hope. Like the promise of spring celebrated in the coldest days of winter or even in the heat of burning sands, faith gains new confidence that God is working in mysterious ways. God watches and waits for us to grasp the good news: I am with you in all the seasons of life. We need not be afraid.

When we finally see spring waters begin to flow, we can announce with joy that God has always been with us, even in times when we wait on mysterious and unexpected surprises to be revealed.

Prayer

Encourage us, God-with-us, to overcome our fears through the power of your living word. Amen.

December 15

Isaiah 35:8, 10
A highway shall be there,
and it shall be called the Holy Way; ...
no traveler, not even fools, shall go astray. ...
And the ransomed of the Lord shall return
and come to Zion with singing;
everlasting joy shall be upon their heads;
they shall obtain joy and gladness,
and sorrow and sighing shall flee away.

To ponder
Open now thy gates of beauty,
Zion, let me enter there,
where my soul in joyful duty

34

waits for God who answers prayer.
Oh, how blessed is this place,
filled with solace, light, and grace!
—"Open now thy gates of beauty," ELW 533

When sorrows flee away

Centuries before the birth of Jesus, exiles returned from Babylon to Jerusalem and the temple. Today's reading from Isaiah 35 and the hymn stanza describe the people's joy at returning home.

We may get a taste of this kind of joy at Christmas worship services, family reunions, and other holiday events that bring us together with friends and loved ones. We know, however, that all will not be merry and bright for everyone. Too many people have no place to call home; too many families, communities, and churches are broken.

But just as God remembered the exiles in Babylon and brought them home again, God is still in the business of hearing and answering prayers, setting people free, and bringing broken relationships and communities back together again.

Prayer

Holy One, comfort and strengthen all who are far from friends or loved ones. Bring reconciliation, healing, and peace to every corner of the earth. Amen.

December 16

Matthew 1:1-6

An account of the genealogy of Jesus the Messiah, the son of David, the son of Abraham.

    Abraham was the father of Isaac, and Isaac the father of Jacob, and Jacob the father of Judah and his brothers, and Judah the father of Perez and Zerah by Tamar, and Perez the father of Hezron, and Hezron the father of Aram, and Aram the father of Aminadab, and Aminadab the father of Nahshon, and Nahshon the father of Salmon, and Salmon the father of Boaz by Rahab, and Boaz the father of Obed by Ruth, and Obed the father of Jesse, and Jesse the father of King David.

To ponder

I had applied for and received a grant to go to South Africa ... [where we] studied culture and reconciliation—a subject for which post-apartheid South Africa had become a living laboratory.—Wes Moore, *The Other Wes Moore*

Embrace the person you are still becoming

Each of the gospels begins in a unique way. The Gospel of Matthew begins with a lengthy genealogy that traces Jesus' ancestors all the way back to Abraham. God had promised that Abraham and Sarah would have descendants and land, and through them all people would be blessed (Genesis 12). In effect, Matthew connects Jesus to this promise.

This detailed family history also shows Jesus' strong roots in Jewish faith and life. If possible, find time to talk with your elders about where your family has roots, and tell stories about your ancestors that show God's grace and blessings. Share with those much younger than you. Then pause to reflect: How has your family history impacted your life? Are there roots or branches you want to explore or develop further? What will you leave behind, and what will you carry into the "living laboratory" of your life and faith, and the person you are still becoming?

Prayer

Spirit of the living God, fall afresh on me. Mold me in your grace and use me to share your love. Amen.

December 17

Matthew 1:7, 10-11

And David was the father of Solomon by the wife of Uriah, and Solomon the father of Rehoboam, and Rehoboam the father of Abijah, and Abijah the father of Asaph, . . . and Hezekiah the father of Manasseh, and Manasseh the father of Amos, and Amos the father of Josiah, and Josiah the father of Jechoniah and his brothers, at the time of the deportation to Babylon.

To ponder

If the fulfillment of every promise or plan rests on God's approval, then God's hand is hidden in everything that happens. According to my grandfather, all tragedy or blessing was a part of some unknowable and dynamic purpose. . . . At any given time, the will of God might be unknown, but the presence of God was certain.—Rachel Naomi Remen, *My Grandfather's Blessings*

Unlikely people, unlikely outcomes

The most well-known ancestors in today's portion of Jesus' genealogy are probably David and his son Solomon. David is known for defeating Goliath, a much larger opponent, and for perhaps being Israel's greatest king. However, David sent a man named Uriah into the front lines of battle so that he could take Uriah's wife, Bathsheba, as his own. David and Bathsheba became the parents of Solomon, who succeeded David on the throne and had a reputation for being wise.

The list of Jesus' ancestors moves on from David and Solomon, until we read that at the time when Josiah had a family, there was a deportation to Babylon. It seems the family history could have ended right there, but it didn't. The people remained in exile for about sixty years, then Cyrus of Persia came into power and allowed them to return home.

God was at work through unlikely people like King David, Persian ruler Cyrus, and many more. Where do you see God at work in the world today?

Prayer

Rekindle our faith, God, and help us to recognize your redeeming love at work in the world. Amen.

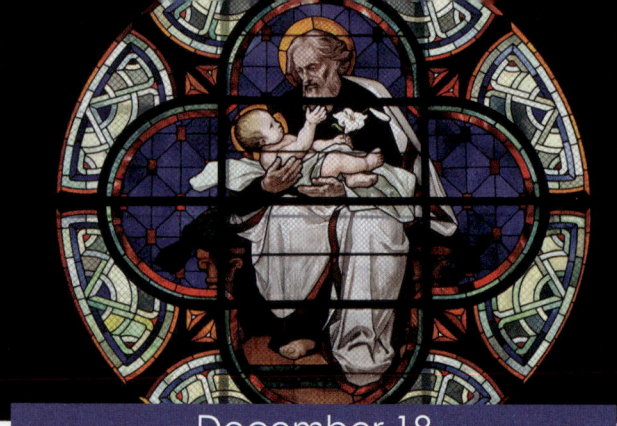

December 18

Matthew 1:12, 16-17

And after the deportation to Babylon: Jechoniah was the father of Salathiel, and Salathiel the father of Zerubbabel, . . . and Jacob the father of Joseph the husband of Mary, who bore Jesus, who is called the Messiah.

So all the generations from Abraham to David are fourteen generations; and from David to the deportation to Babylon, fourteen generations; and from the deportation to Babylon to the Messiah, fourteen generations.

To ponder

My own parents seemed to have no interest in the suburbs and whatever toehold they might provide. Their choice was to keep us rooted in our community, close to aunts, uncles, grandparents, and cousins.... We were comfortable inside the mix of people, the range of races, class, and culture that existed around us. That mix was shelter. For us, it was never anything but good.—Michelle Obama, *The Light We Carry*

A good mix of people

At last, in Jesus' genealogy list in Matthew, we come to Joseph and Mary! This list follows the family line from Abraham all the way to Joseph. As we will see in the next few days, Matthew's nativity story also focuses on Joseph, especially in comparison to the Gospel of Luke, where Mary is a more central character.

Matthew has detailed 42 generations that connect Jesus to Abraham and Sarah and God's promises to them and show Jesus' deep roots in Jewish faith and life. As it is for each of us, these ancestors are sometimes unlikely, sometimes remarkable (yet fallible) human beings.

What "mix of people"—friends and family members—remind you of God's goodness and grace?

Prayer

God of the past, present, and future, thank you for your promises and for people who remind me of your faithfulness. Amen.

December 19

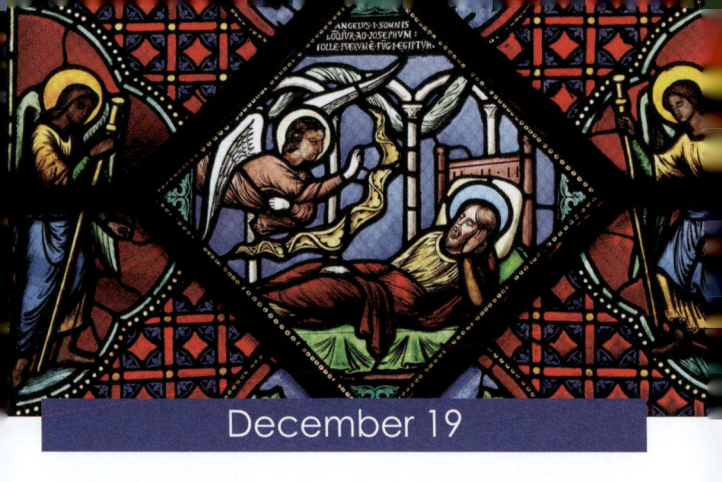

Matthew 1:18-21

Now the birth of Jesus the Messiah took place in this way. When his mother Mary had been engaged to Joseph, but before they lived together, she was found to be pregnant from the Holy Spirit. Her husband Joseph, being a righteous man and unwilling to expose her to public disgrace, planned to divorce her quietly. But just when he had resolved to do this, an angel of the Lord appeared to him in a dream and said, "Joseph, son of David, do not be afraid to take Mary as your wife, for the child conceived in her is from the Holy Spirit. She will bear a son, and you are to name him Jesus, for he will save his people from their sins."

To ponder
Come, thou long-expected Jesus,
born to set thy people free;
from our fears and sins release us;
let us find our rest in thee.
Israel's strength and consolation,
hope of all the earth thou art,
dear desire of every nation,
joy of every longing heart.
—"Come, thou long-expected Jesus," ELW 254

An angelic intervention
When Joseph, seeing no other options, makes the difficult decision to "quietly" divorce Mary, God sends an angel to speak to him. This angel reveals more information about what is happening—and gives the baby a name.

Left to ourselves, our decisions are limited by what we see and know, but God may have something surprising in store for us. Pray and watch for ways that God's grace might be unfolding in each day. Rejoice in the possibilities of what the holy days ahead may reveal—tidings of comfort and joy that we cannot ignore.

Prayer
God of hope and surprise, help us recognize the remarkable ways your grace unfolds all around us. Amen.

December 20

Matthew 1:22-23

All this took place to fulfill what had been spoken by the Lord through the prophet:

"Look, the virgin shall become pregnant and give birth to a son, and they shall name him Emmanuel," which means, "God is with us."

To ponder

Do images of Jesus offer reassurance and neurological stimulation? Do they fulfil a theological quest? Are they a natural result of an incarnational theology or a desire to have a personal relationship with the Divine? Are they less a window into Jesus than a reflection of ourselves? . . . Yes. But the hows and whys are complicated. Of this though, I'm certain: when we gaze on an image of Jesus, there is so much more going on than meets the eye.—Trisha Elliott, "The Many Faces of Jesus"

The many faces of Jesus

How would you portray the face of the Christ child, Emmanuel, God-with-us in a painting, photo, or nativity scene?

Clearly there is no one way to present the baby Jesus. Over the years, many portrayals of Jesus' face simply reflected the face of the artist, who was often white. More recently, I have been inspired by multicultural portrayals of Jesus that remind us that God is with us—every one of us.

Allow your journey through these holy days to be enriched by a variety of ways of portraying the one named Emmanuel, God-with-us.

Prayer

Giver of joy and peace, help us to see your face in new ways—and let the wonders of diversity bring both justice and joy to this world. Amen.

December 21 / Advent 4

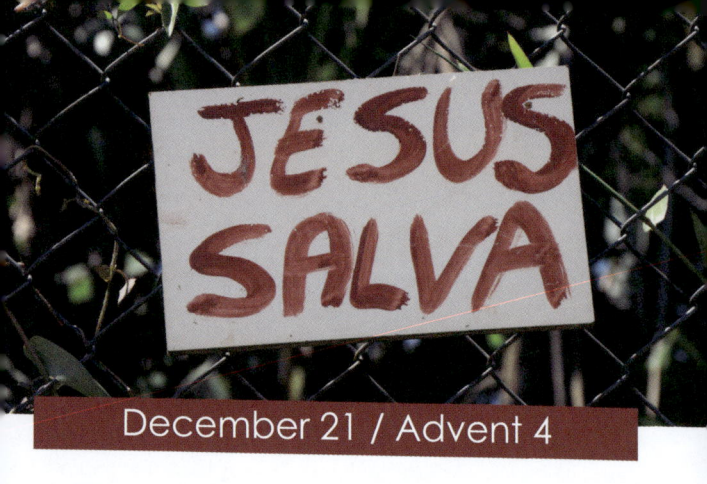

Matthew 1:24-25
When Joseph awoke from sleep, he did as the angel of the Lord commanded him; he took her as his wife but had no marital relations with her until she had given birth to a son, and he named him Jesus.

To ponder
Life in Jesus Christ rightly hopes for "all things, whether on earth or in heaven" . . . , believing that all things have peace in his cross. Jesus Christ is God come within our limits. He brings about the transformation of the limited place itself to become the place of grace, praise, and compassion.
—Gordon W. Lathrop, *Holy Things*

Jesus saves

Joseph follows through on what the angel in his dream told him to do. He takes Mary as his wife and names the newborn baby. Nearly hidden in this brief account from Matthew is a powerful announcement: Jesus our Savior is born!

The name *Jesus* was fairly common among Jews at the time. It has Hebrew roots in the name *Yeshua*, meaning "Yahweh saves" or "The Lord is salvation." This name is a reminder that Jesus came to bring salvation to the world through his life, death, and resurrection.

Jesús salva. Jesus saves. No matter what language we speak, let us honor the name of Jesus and his power to love, forgive, save, and make all things new.

Prayer

Jesus, you are our salvation. Come into our lives and into the world today with your saving power and peace. Amen.

December 22

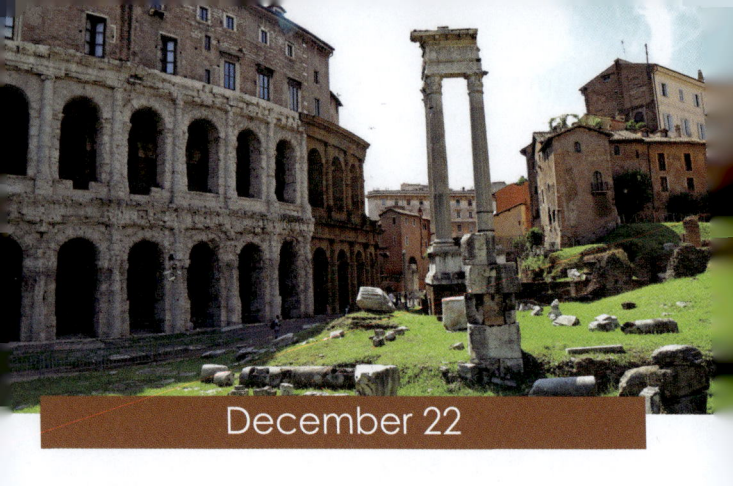

Luke 2:1-3
In those days a decree went out from Caesar Augustus that all the world should be registered. This was the first registration and was taken while Quirinius was governor of Syria. All went to their own towns to be registered.

To ponder
Only in the empire are we pressed and urged and invited to pretend that things are all right—either in the dean's office or in our marriage or in the hospital room. And as long as the empire can keep the pretense alive that things are all right, there will be no real grieving and no serious criticism.—Walter Brueggemann, *The Prophetic Imagination*

Main characters in God's story

This story begins with empire. Caesar Augustus is the Roman emperor; Quirinius is a middle-management governor of Syria. These are men of power, wealth, and main-character energy. Registration is a tool of empire to control, tax, or gain allegiance. The empire seems to be the point of the story. But Luke has other ideas.

Theologian Walter Brueggemann notes that people of faith are often at odds with empire. The prophets demonstrate this tension in the Old Testament; Jesus picks up the theme in his opposition to those who value output, acquisition, and power.

In contrast to the destructive (yet seductive) power of empire, Brueggemann offers prophetic imagination: casting an alternative vision aligned with the reign of God. This vision might include a young woman who bears the son of God, a humble carpenter who trusts God through a scandal, and shepherds who are the first to receive the news of Jesus' birth.

Luke's introduction to the incarnation story locates us in time with the empire of the day, but we will soon see that the main characters in God's story don't need power, fame, influence, or wealth. The main characters in God's story are those who at any time have felt like the least, the lost, or the lonely.

Prayer

Mighty God, deliver us from the empty promises of empire and inspire us to live out your reign of justice and love. Amen.

December 23

Luke 2:4-5
Joseph also went from the town of Nazareth in Galilee to Judea, to the city of David called Bethlehem, because he was descended from the house and family of David. He went to be registered with Mary, to whom he was engaged and who was expecting a child.

To ponder
Stony the road we trod, bitter the chast'ning rod,
felt in the days when hope unborn had died;
yet with a steady beat, have not our weary feet
come to the place for which our parents sighed?
—"Lift every voice and sing," ELW 841

Along the way

Imagine Mary and Joseph as reluctant, weary travelers on the four-day journey (in those days) from Nazareth to Bethlehem, about 90 miles. They must have known that the baby could come at any moment, yet they traveled nonetheless, and not exactly in comfort. Some journeys are like this: reluctant, tedious, nerve-wracking. Sometimes you travel for pleasure. Sometimes you travel to help a loved one, to seek a better life, to survive, or because the government tells you to go.

This is the last day of Advent. How was your Advent journey? A gently winding road with pleasant side trips? A breakneck race to get ready for Christmas? A journey of grief anticipating the first holiday without a loved one? A journey of change as a life transition approaches? We too are on journeys—some that we long to take, and some that we hoped we'd never have to endure.

Mary and Joseph's journey brought fear, pain, surprise, and joy. Yet God kept showing up—in the shepherds who received the angels' good news, and in a vulnerable infant. The same is true of our journeys. God shows up along the way. There is no road we can take where God will not accompany us.

Prayer

Constant Friend, thank you for journeying with us all the days of our lives. Be with all who journey in fear this day. Help us to recognize you in every person we meet. Amen.

December 24 / Christmas Eve

Luke 2:6-7
While they were there, the time came for her to deliver her child. And she gave birth to her firstborn son and wrapped him in bands of cloth and laid him in a manger, because there was no place in the guest room.

To ponder
According to Luke, God enters history in the person of Christ to effect a liberating revolution in human relationships. Mary is exalted because, through her, God will work this revolution in history. . . . She makes it possible through her act of faith, but the liberating action of God in history liberates her. She herself embodies and personifies the oppressed and subjugated

people who are being liberated and exalted through God's redemptive power.—Rosemary Radford Reuther, *Sexism and God-Talk*

Humble and holy

We have entered the delivery room with Mary, and, for a moment, it is all about her. Set aside the powerful rulers named earlier in Luke's story—and even Joseph.

In Luke's Christmas story, Mary is centered. Her experience is relevant. Her actions matter. She is to be celebrated for her power, courage, and caretaking. What does it mean to make this young woman a central character in a story about the Son of God? There are other ways this story could be told without mentioning a birth, swaddling clothes, a manger.

Jesus came to earth in humility, which centers those who have for too long been at the margins. What does it mean to focus on those who are left behind, powerless, suffering, or invisible? We may be called to enter spaces that are uncomfortable or unfamiliar. We might be invited to listen to voices that we have overlooked. But first, we sit with Mary, the God-bearer, in wonder and awe. Through her, Christ has come to us all.

Prayer

Holy child, instill in us gratitude for your humble appearance and openness to care for those who have been on the margins. Amen.

December 25 / Christmas Day

Luke 2:8-12
Now in that same region there were shepherds living in the fields, keeping watch over their flock by night. Then an angel of the Lord stood before them, and the glory of the Lord shone around them, and they were terrified. But the angel said to them, "Do not be afraid, for see, I am bringing you good news of great joy for all the people: to you is born this day in the city of David a Savior, who is the Messiah, the Lord. This will be a sign for you: you will find a child wrapped in bands of cloth and lying in a manger."

To ponder
The whole climate of the gospel is a continual demand for the right of the poor to make themselves heard, to be considered

preferentially by society.... Was not Christ's first preaching to "proclaim the liberation of the oppressed"?—Gustavo Gutiérrez, *A Theology of Liberation*

Celebrate the good news!

As a reporter at a daily newspaper, it was my job to write the news. One of the hardest things about writing the news was to write just the news. I was not to label the news as good news, bad news, or fake news. From school board meetings to new meat packing plants, neutral news reporting was key.

The Christmas angel brings news, but not just any news. This is the news for which God's people have been waiting. This news is biased; the gospel writer takes a side. Luke reports that this "good news of great joy" tosses the powerful from their thrones and lifts up the lowly (1:52). It means relief for those who are poor and freedom for those who are oppressed (4:18).

The Savior has come for you and for all people. This news is trustworthy. This news reorients us toward the love of God and the love of neighbor, and brings joy to the world and all creation. What good news to celebrate and share!

Prayer

Christ our Savior, help us to receive, celebrate, and embody the good news of your coming. Amen.

December 26

Luke 2:13-14
And suddenly there was with the angel a multitude of the heavenly host, praising God and saying, "Glory to God in the highest heaven, and on earth peace among those whom he favors!"

To ponder
We are showered every day with gifts, but they are not meant for us to keep. Their life is in their movement, the inhale and the exhale of our shared breath. Our work and our joy is to pass along the gift and to trust that what we put out into the universe will always come back.—Robin Wall Kimmerer, *Braiding Sweetgrass*

A gift for us to give away

Many in the United Kingdom celebrate today as Boxing Day, based on a centuries-old tradition of gifts given on this day to tradespeople, employees, and servants. December 26 is also the feast day for Stephen, a New Testament deacon who distributed food and resources to those in need. He was later stoned to death; some in the early church marked this day by collecting alms for the poor.

We might be a little tired of gift-giving by now. After everything is unwrapped, tried on, and assembled, what's left of Christmas? The angels' words speak into our post-Christmas haze with a gift that cannot be wrapped and cannot be returned: the presence and peace of God. This gift is intangible. You can't see the angels' praise, you cannot empirically document God's peace. But this gift of the angel proclamation satisfies our longings in a way that no gadget can. God is here among us. God brings peace to surround us. The proper response to such a gift is to keep giving it away.

Prayer

Generous God, among the trappings of this season, grant us wisdom to receive the gifts you bring. Help us share those gifts with those in need. Amen.

December 27

Luke 2:16-20

So [the shepherds] went with haste and found Mary and Joseph and the child lying in the manger. When they saw this, they made known what had been told them about this child, and all who heard it were amazed at what the shepherds told them, and Mary treasured all these words and pondered them in her heart. The shepherds returned, glorifying and praising God for all they had heard and seen, just as it had been told them.

To ponder

In fact, Mary and Joseph only hear of angelic activity because the shepherds tell them. Could it be that we who feel responsible for giving birth to the Christ child or to Christmas or to

58

Christmas worship will receive the good news of great joy not from angelic inspiration but from someone sent to us from out in the field?—Craig Satterlee, "Commentary on Luke 2:1-14 [15-20]"

Unexpected messengers

Now it is the shepherds' moment. They are ordinary people working the night shift. They do not have prestige, education, or power. It is another Christmas miracle: God's angels came first to the humble shepherds, while they were on the job, with the good news of the incarnation. We might think they had no right to hear first. Surely it should have been someone more important, more religious. We may be amazed that the shepherds hear the good news first, but it is even more amazing that others believed them.

The shepherds are transformed from guys in a field to evangelists and worshipers. An encounter with God can do that. If an ordinary shepherd can be transformed by a holy encounter, then so can we. We might encounter God on any given day at work, school, or home. Just as likely, someone unexpected will bear the good news to us. Keep alert! A word from God can come from anywhere and anyone—right out of left field.

Prayer

Surprising God, we marvel at your presence—everywhere! Humble us to experience your truth from unexpected messengers. Amen.

December 28 / The Holy Innocents

Matthew 2:13-15

An angel of the Lord appeared to Joseph in a dream and said, "Get up, take the child and his mother, and flee to Egypt, and remain there until I tell you, for Herod is about to search for the child, to destroy him." Then Joseph got up, took the child and his mother by night, and went to Egypt and remained there until the death of Herod. This was to fulfill what had been spoken by the Lord through the prophet, "Out of Egypt I have called my son."

To ponder

Children who move from their home country to another country as refugees (because it was not safe for them to stay there) should get help and protection and have the same rights as children born in that country.—United Nations Convention on the Rights of the Child: The Children's Version

Holy refugees

For most of us it is nearly impossible to imagine having to flee your home and move to a new land to escape persecution and to protect your family. But because Joseph listened to the angel's message and acted with courage, he, Mary, and the child Jesus found safe refuge in Egypt. People there must have welcomed them and shown them hospitality. Imagine if they had not—this family of three may have had to return to Judea and face Herod's violence.

Global Refuge (formerly Lutheran Immigration and Refugee Services) helps families fleeing the dangers of war, persecution, and disaster to find a new and safe home elsewhere. It takes many caring people in host countries to welcome and help settle refugee families. Christians welcome refugees and other vulnerable people knowing that Jesus himself was a child refugee needing safety.

Prayer

O Lord, protect all innocent ones who need safety, sustenance, and a place to call home. Open our hearts to the needs of refugees and inspire our churches to care for others the way Joseph cared for Jesus, offering protection and loving care. Amen.

December 29

Matthew 2:16-18

When Herod saw that he had been tricked by the magi, he was infuriated, and he sent and killed all the children in and around Bethlehem who were two years old or under, according to the time that he had learned from the magi. Then what had been spoken through the prophet Jeremiah was fulfilled:
"A voice was heard in Ramah,
wailing and loud lamentation,
Rachel weeping for her children;
she refused to be consoled, because they are no more."

To ponder

We all need permission in our grief to fall apart sometimes, permission to lose all decorum, permission to name how truly

awful and terrifying death can be and how shattered we are.—
Amanda Held Opelt, *Keening*

Unconsolable

Matthew quotes Jeremiah to describe the intense grief that must have been felt by all the parents of the children slaughtered by Herod. We are often uncomfortable with such raw expressions of pain and grief. We might be tempted to seek to quickly console those who are going through inexpressible sorrow and anguish, such as at the death of a child. Consolation does not come quickly or cheaply at such terrible loss. First, pain and grief must be expressed, even with wailing and loud lamentation.

The church and friends of the bereaved can create spaces where such uninhibited expressions of grief are accepted, named, and not quickly consoled. To do so requires becoming comfortable with the uncomfortable. It requires faith that the God of all tears, the God of the crucified Jesus, is present in and shares our pain and sorrow.

Prayer

God of compassion, I pray for all those whose grief is too great to bear. Grant me a listening ear and a patient heart as I encounter all who mourn during this Christmas season. Amen.

December 30

Matthew 2:19-21
When Herod died, an angel of the Lord suddenly appeared in a dream to Joseph in Egypt and said, "Get up, take the child and his mother, and go to the land of Israel, for those who were seeking the child's life are dead."

Then Joseph got up, took the child and his mother, and went to the land of Israel.

To ponder
It is said an Eastern monarch once charged his wise men to invent him a sentence, to be ever in view, and which should be true and appropriate in all times and situations. They pre-

sented him the words: "And this, too, shall pass away." How much it expresses! How chastening in the hour of pride!—how consoling in the depths of affliction! "And this, too, shall pass away." And yet let us hope it is not quite true. Let us hope, rather, that . . . we shall secure an individual, social, and political prosperity and happiness, whose course shall be onward and upward, and which, while the earth endures, shall not pass away.—Abraham Lincoln, "Address before the Wisconsin State Agricultural Society"

This too shall pass

There is some comfort in knowing that Herod's reign of terror—like that of all tyrants and oppressive rulers—did not last forever, giving Joseph, Mary, and the child Jesus a new hope.

We may live through difficult, even oppressive, times when it seems that suffering in our world will never end. The birth of Jesus is a reminder that his reign of peace is the only kingdom that endures.

We can find comfort in communities of faith that acknowledge the suffering in our world, find strength together to endure, and receive hope and courage to work for that reign of Christ that is eternal.

Prayer

Merciful God, even as we face hard times, give us faith to look for your reign of peace among us now in Christ Jesus. Amen.

December 31

Matthew 2:22-23

But when [Joseph] heard that Archelaus was ruling Judea in place of his father Herod, he was afraid to go there. And after being warned in a dream, he went away to the district of Galilee.

There he made his home in a town called Nazareth, so that what had been spoken through the prophets might be fulfilled, "He will be called a Nazarene."

To ponder

You can't go back home to your family, back home to your childhood, ... away from all the strife and conflict of the world, back home to the father you have lost and have been looking for, back home to someone who can help you, save you, ease the burden for you, back home to the old forms and systems of things which once seemed everlasting but which are changing all the time—back home to the escapes of Time and Memory.—Thomas Wolfe, *You Can't Go Home Again*

You can't go home again

Joseph, Mary, and the child Jesus were on a difficult journey. Perhaps they assumed that after the danger was over in Jerusalem they could go back home and enjoy their old life. Instead, Joseph learned in a dream that the danger was still real, so he led his family to start a new life in a new home.

Have you ever had to start over in a new place because you couldn't go back home? Have you ever moved away and then returned to your hometown, but everything was so different it didn't feel like home anymore? Some people are rejected by family, and they have no place to call home.

Joseph trusted that God was with him as he led his family to a new life in a new place. When we face the sadness of losing home and accept the challenge of starting over in a new place, we can know that God travels with us and watches over us in every new place. God is always at home with us.

Prayer

O God, in every day and every place, help us trust that you are our home through Jesus Christ. Amen.

January 1 / Name of Jesus

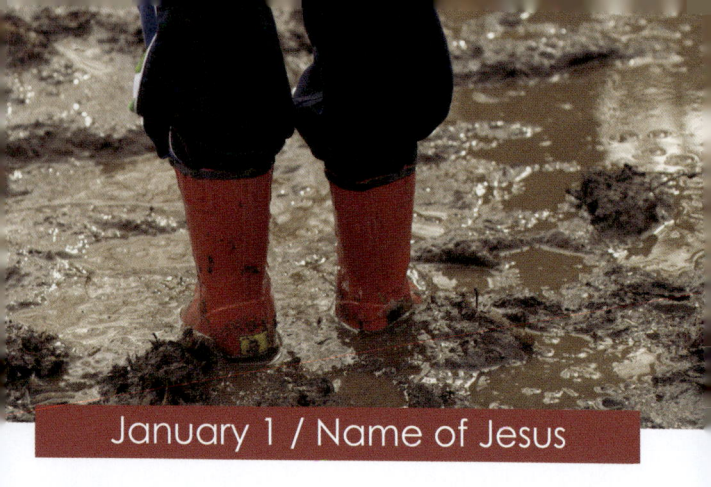

Philippians 2:7-11
And being found in appearance as a human,
he humbled himself
and became obedient to the point of death—
even death on a cross.
Therefore God exalted him even more highly
and gave him the name
that is above every other name,
so that at the name given to Jesus
every knee should bend,
in heaven and on earth and under the earth,
and every tongue should confess
that Jesus Christ is Lord,
to the glory of God the Father.

To ponder

In a lowly manger born, humble life begun in scorn;
under Joseph's watchful eye, Jesus grew as you and I;
knew the suff'rings of the weak,
knew the patience of the meek,
hungered as but poor folk can; this is he. Behold the man!
—"In a lowly manger born," ELW 718

Humble human humus humor

God exalts Jesus' humility and willingness to let go of power and privilege. We, however, find it difficult to embrace humility in our lives. We may fear others will think less of us. We might cling to our accomplishments and prestige to feel good about ourselves, or perhaps to feel worthy of God's love.

Jesus chooses a different path. He embraces the fullness of being human. To be human is to be connected to the ground, to the earth. God created the first human "from the dust of the ground" (Genesis 2:6), after all. To be humble is to accept our full human, earthy reality.

Humility often goes along with a wonderful sense of humor. Our ability to laugh at ourselves, especially our mistakes and limitations, is a joyful expression of the humility we share with each other in Christ.

Prayer

Lord Jesus, help me embrace my own humble life as you embrace us all just as we are. Amen.

January 2

Matthew 2:1-2

In the time of King Herod, after Jesus was born in Bethlehem of Judea, magi from the east came to Jerusalem, asking, "Where is the child who has been born king of the Jews? For we observed his star in the east and have come to pay him homage."

To ponder

Our bodies are entire universes made up of stories.... How we choose to share them can look as different and as vast as stars in the night sky.—Jenny Sung, *Call to Allyship*

Starstruck

I was about twelve years old when I went to my first official concert with my sister, Chrystal, and a friend from school. It was New Edition on their "Candy Girl" tour in 1983. (New Edition was the equivalent of the Beatles or Beyoncé, depending on your birthday.) Still today, in my fifties, many concerts later, I remember the excitement, the anticipation, and of course feeling like a certified teenager. No question, I was starstruck.

Perhaps the magi experienced a similar version of being starstruck. They were experts on the courses of the stars. They understood astrology and recognized that this star was like no other. This star was leading them to the fulfillment of prophecy, to the newborn king. They were compelled to follow with gifts suited for royalty.

We are not certain how many magi were present. But we are certain that the birth of the Christ child beckons beyond geography, religion, and customs. What does that mean for us today?

Prayer

God of the universe, you know each star by name. Thank you for the bright star that leads us to the babe in the manger and the Savior of the galaxy. Amen.

January 3

Matthew 2:3-6

When King Herod heard this, he was frightened, and all Jerusalem with him, and calling together all the chief priests and scribes of the people, he inquired of them where the Messiah was to be born. They told him, "In Bethlehem of Judea, for so it has been written by the prophet:
'And you, Bethlehem, in the land of Judah,
are by no means least among the rulers of Judah,
for from you shall come a ruler
who is to shepherd my people Israel.'"

To ponder

And so, through all the length of days,
thy goodness faileth never.

Good Shepherd, may I sing thy praise
within thy house forever.
—"The King of love my shepherd is," ELW 502

Good Shepherd

Many titles await this babe in the manger: Messiah, Bread of life, King of the Jews, Prince of peace, True Vine, Lily of the valley, and certainly, Good Shepherd.

When I hear the word *shepherd*, I think about Psalm 23 and find myself humming one of my favorite hymns, "The King of love my shepherd is." In biblical times shepherds lived without notoriety or wealth, spending days and nights with their flocks. What does it mean for us that the birth of the Christ child was revealed to shepherds?

The good news for us today is the same good news from the very first Christmas: Be not afraid! Unto us a child is born, unto us a Son is given. There is no single word, symbol, or metaphor that can completely capture all of who Jesus is, but what we do know is that we serve the God of the universe— the indescribable, uncontainable, unfathomable God—and yes, this God is our faithful and loving Good Shepherd.

Prayer

Good Shepherd, thank you for being present with us, especially in the valleys of despair. We trust that you are the Alpha and the Omega, the beginning and the end. Our lives are in your hands, and we are thankful. Amen.

January 4 / Christmas 2

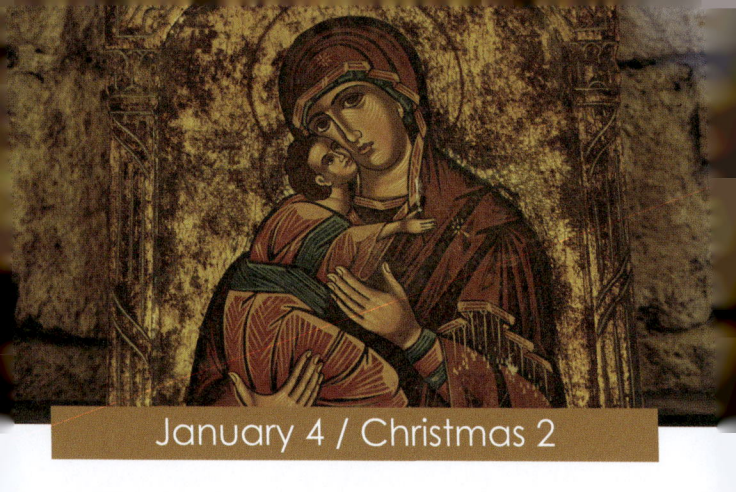

Matthew 2:7-8
Herod secretly called for the magi and learned from them the exact time when the star had appeared. Then he sent them to Bethlehem, saying, "Go and search diligently for the child, and when you have found him, bring me word so that I may also go and pay him homage."

To ponder
Maybe God is trying to tell you something.—Alice Walker, *The Color Purple*

Hidden

It was Christmas Eve. My older sister Chrystal and I stood at the door, awestruck: Was Santa Claus actually in our house? Let's see. Red hat? Check. White beard? Check. Red Santa suit? Check. Gifts galore? Check. That settles it. It's Santa.

I thought I was witnessing a miracle. In my heart I shouted, "I've been a good girl all year!" There was no way I could contain my enthusiasm. I announced aloud that somebody should get Dad. Chrystal did not miss a beat. She said, "Angie, that is Dad."

My mind was instantly altered. Could she be right? What does this mean? Our dad is Santa Claus? I could not believe my eyes. Having Santa at our house was one of the most exciting moments of my life. Even now, decades later, I can still feel my heart flutter with amazement. This was a truth I was not prepared to accept.

King Herod was not prepared to accept a newborn king of the Jews. Is there a truth you do not wish to acknowledge? What truth could empower you and others?

Prayer

Thank you, God, for your Holy Spirit that leads us to all truth. Please prepare our hearts to receive your wisdom so that we may live into our baptismal calling to be your disciples. Amen.

January 5

Matthew 2:9-11

When [the magi] had heard the king, they set out, and there, ahead of them, went the star that they had seen in the east, until it stopped over the place where the child was. When they saw that the star had stopped, they were overwhelmed with joy. On entering the house, they saw the child with Mary his mother, and they knelt down and paid him homage. Then, opening their treasure chests, they offered him gifts of gold, frankincense, and myrrh.

To ponder

Down in a lonely manger
the humble Christ was born;
and God sent us salvation

that blessed Christmas morn.
Go tell it on the mountain,
over the hills and everywhere;
go tell it on the mountain
that Jesus Christ is born!
—"Go tell it on the mountain," *This Far by Faith* 52

The gift of hope

God chose to enter humanity through an unwed teenage mother, in the muck and filth of a stable. God chose to show up just where we would least expect God to be. God does not come to the world's center to rule in power and might, but rather, Jesus is born on the fringe of society to make a new beginning altogether. Jesus is born not to make us more comfortable, but to overturn tables, to resurrect and redeem us. In a world strangled by division and hate, we have the gift of hope!

The peace that Jesus gives is not the peace from a military ruler; this king is not a leader of power like Herod or Caesar. This is not good news just for the rich and connected; this is not a kingdom that will pass into history. The Christ child brings love, hope, and justice for all and forever.

Prayer

Dear God, the world is starving for meaning, for direction, for hope. Thank you for guiding us as we continue to follow you on our faith journey. Amen.

January 6 / Epiphany of Our Lord

Matthew 2:12
And having been warned in a dream not to return to Herod, they left for their own country by another road.

To ponder
The spirit of God dwells in the holy darkness where we are invited to be held in God's love. —Sharei Green and Beckah Selnick, *God's Holy Darkness*

Holy darkness
Epiphany marks the end of the Christmas season and commemorates the magi coming from afar to pay homage to the Christ child. The liturgical color for the day is white, and the

time after Epiphany is often associated with all things white, light, and bright. Yet the star guiding the magi appeared to them in the sacred darkness of night, and they took a different way home after they were warned in a dream not to return to King Herod. In another dream, Joseph was warned to flee to Egypt with the holy family.

God does amazing work in darkness: "Darkness and blackness are too often compared to lightness and whiteness and day and found deficient, but let us name the beauty and goodness and holiness of darkness and blackness and night" (Green and Selnick, *God's Holy Darkness*). Life begins in darkness. The darkness of the earth and the darkness of the womb both hold life. Jesus was covered by darkness in Mary's womb.

Can you think of other examples of God's activity in and through holy darkness?

Prayer
Thank you, God, for the beauty of holy darkness. Help us to remember that the night is part of your good creation and to trust your presence in midnight moments. Amen.

Household Blessings and Prayers

Advent

In the days of Advent, Christians prepare to celebrate the presence of God's Word among us in our own day. During these four weeks, we pray that the reign of God, which Jesus preached and lived, would come among us. We pray that God's justice would flourish in our land, that the people of the earth would live in peace, that the weak and the sick and the hungry would be strengthened, healed, and fed with God's merciful presence.

During the last days of Advent, Christians welcome Christ with names inspired by the prophets: wisdom, liberator of slaves, mighty power, radiant dawn and sun of justice, the keystone of the arch of humanity, and Emmanuel—God with us.

The Advent wreath

One of the best-known customs for the season is the Advent wreath. The wreath and winter candle-lighting in the midst of growing darkness strengthen some of the Advent images found in the Bible. The unbroken circle of greens is clearly an image of everlasting life, a victory wreath, the crown of Christ, or the wheel of time itself. Christians use the wreath as a sign that Christ reaches into our time to lead us to the light of everlasting life. The four candles mark the progress of the four weeks of Advent and the growth of light. Sometimes the wreath is embellished with natural dried flowers or fruit. Its evergreen branches lead the household and the congregation to the evergreen Christmas tree. In many homes, the family gathers for prayer around the wreath.

An evening service of light for Advent

This brief order may be used on any evening during the season of Advent. If the household has an Advent wreath (one candle for each of the four weeks of Advent), it may be lighted during this service. Alternatively, one simple candle (perhaps a votive candle) may be lighted instead.

Lighting the Advent wreath
May this candle/these candles be a sign of the coming light of Christ.
One or more candles may be lighted.

Week 1: Lighting the first candle
Blessed are you, God of Jacob, for you promise to transform weapons of war into implements of planting and harvest and to teach us your way of peace; you promise that our night of sin is far gone and that your day of salvation is dawning.

As we light the first Advent candle, wake us from our sleep, wrap us in your light, empower us to live honorably, and guide us along your path of peace.

O house of Jacob, come,
let us walk in the light of the Lord. Amen.

Week 2: Lighting the first two candles
Blessed are you, God of hope, for you promise to bring forth a shoot from the stump of Jesse who will bring justice to the poor, who will deliver the needy and crush the oppressor, who will stand as a signal of hope for all people.

As we light these candles, turn our wills to bear the fruit of repentance, transform our hearts to live in justice and harmony with one another, and fix our eyes on the shoot from Jesse, Jesus Christ, the hope of all nations.

O people of hope, come,
let us rejoice in the faithfulness of the Lord. Amen.

Week 3: Lighting three candles
Blessed are you, God of might and majesty, for you promise to make the desert rejoice and blossom, to watch over the strangers, and to set the prisoners free.

As we light these candles, satisfy our hunger with your good gifts, open our eyes to the great things you have done for us, and fill us with patience until the coming of the Lord Jesus.

O ransomed people of the Lord, come,
let us travel on God's holy way
and enter into Zion with singing. Amen.

Week 4: Lighting all four candles
Blessed are you, God of hosts, for you promised to send a Son, Emmanuel, who brought your presence among us; and you promise through your Son Jesus to save us from our sin.

As we light these candles, turn again to us in mercy; strengthen our faith in the word spoken by your prophets; restore us and give us life that we may be saved.

O house of David, come,
let us rejoice, for the Son of God, Emmanuel,
comes to be with us. Amen.

Reading
Read the scripture passage printed in the devotion for the day.

Hymn

One of the following hymns may be sung. The hymn might be accompanied by small finger cymbals.

"Light one candle to watch for Messiah," ELW 240
"People, look east," ELW 248
"Savior of the nations, come," ELW 263

During the final seven days of the Advent season (beginning December 17), the hymn "O come, O come, Emmanuel" (ELW 257) is particularly appropriate. The first stanza of the hymn could be sung each day during the final days before Christmas in addition to the stanza that is specifically appointed for the day.

First stanza
O come, O come, Emmanuel,
and ransom captive Israel,
that mourns in lonely exile here
until the Son of God appear.
Refrain Rejoice! Rejoice! Emmanuel shall come to you, O Israel.

December 17
O come, O Wisdom from on high,
embracing all things far and nigh:
in strength and beauty come and stay;
teach us your will and guide our way. *Refrain*

December 18

O come, O come, O Lord of might,
as to your tribes on Sinai's height
in ancient times you gave the law
in cloud, and majesty, and awe. *Refrain*

December 19

O come, O Branch of Jesse, free
your own from Satan's tyranny;
from depths of hell your people save,
and give them vict'ry o'er the grave. *Refrain*

December 20

O come, O Key of David, come,
and open wide our heav'nly home;
make safe the way that leads on high,
and close the path to misery. *Refrain*

December 21

O come, O Dayspring, come and cheer;
O Sun of justice, now draw near.
Disperse the gloomy clouds of night,
and death's dark shadow put to flight. *Refrain*

December 22

O come, O King of nations, come,
O Cornerstone that binds in one:
refresh the hearts that long for you;
restore the broken, make us new. *Refrain*

December 23
O come, O come, Emmanuel,
and ransom captive Israel,
that mourns in lonely exile here
until the Son of God appear. *Refrain*

Text: *Psalteriolum Cantionum Catholicarum*

Table prayer for Advent

Blessed are you, O Lord our God,
the one who is, who was, and who is to come.
At this table you fill us with good things.
May these gifts strengthen us
to share with the hungry and all those in need,
as we wait and watch for your coming among us
in Jesus Christ our Lord. Amen.

Christmas

Over the centuries, various customs have developed that focus the household on welcoming the light of Christ: the daily or weekly lighting of the Advent wreath, the blessing of the lighted Christmas tree, the candlelit procession of Las Posadas, the flickering lights of the luminaria, the Christ candle at Christmas.

The Christian household not only welcomes the light of Christ at Christmas but also celebrates the presence of that light throughout the Twelve Days, from Christmas until the Epiphany, January 6. In the Christmas season, Christians welcome the light of Christ that is already with us through faith. In word and gesture, prayer and song, in the many customs of diverse cultures, Christians celebrate this life-giving Word and ask that it dwell more deeply in the rhythm of daily life.

Lighting the Christmas tree

Use this prayer when you first illumine the tree or when you gather at the tree.

Holy God,
we praise you as we light this tree.
It gives light to this place
as you shine light into darkness through Jesus,
the light of the world.

God of all,
we thank you for your love,
the love that has come to us in Jesus.
Be with us now as we remember that gift of love,
and help us to share that love with a yearning world.
Creator God,
you made the stars in the heavens.
Thank you for the light that shines on us in Jesus,
the bright morning star. Amen.

Blessing of the nativity scene

This blessing may be used when figures are added to the nativity scene and throughout the days of Christmas.

Bless us, O God, as we remember a humble birth. With each angel and shepherd we place here before you, show us the wonder found in a stable. In song and prayer, silence and awe, we adore your gift of love, Christ Jesus our Savior. Amen.

Table prayer for the twelve days of Christmas (December 25–January 5)

With joy and gladness we feast upon your love, O God.
You have come among us in Jesus, your Son,
and your presence now graces this table.
May Christ dwell in us
that we might bear his love to all the world,
for he is Lord forever and ever. Amen.

Epiphany

On the Epiphany of Our Lord (January 6), the household joins the church throughout the world in celebrating the manifestation, the "epiphany," of Christ to the world. The festival of Christmas is thus set within the context of outreach to the larger community; it possesses an outward movement. The festival of the Epiphany asks the Christian household: How might our faith in Christ the Light be shared with friends and family, with our neighbors, with the poor and needy in our land, with those who live in other nations?

Blessing for a home

Matthew writes that when the magi saw the shining star stop overhead, they were filled with joy. "On entering the house, they saw the child with Mary his mother" (Matthew 2:11). In the home, Christ is met in family and friends, in visitors and strangers. In the home, faith is shared, nurtured, and put into action. In the home, Christ is welcome.

Twelfth Night (January 5), Epiphany of Our Lord (January 6), or another day during the time after Epiphany offers an occasion for gathering with friends and family members for a blessing of the home. Someone may lead the greeting and blessing, while another person may read the scripture passage. Following an Eastern European tradition, a visual blessing may be inscribed with white chalk above the main door; for example, 20 + CMB + 26. The numbers change with each new year. The three letters stand for either the ancient Latin blessing Christe mansionem benedicat, *which means "Christ, bless this house," or the legendary names of the magi (Caspar, Melchior, and Balthasar).*

Greeting
Peace to this house and to all who enter here.
By wisdom a house is built,
and by understanding it is established;
by knowledge the rooms are filled
with all precious and pleasant riches. (*Proverbs 24:3-4*)

Reading
As we prepare to ask God's blessing on this household,
let us listen to the words of scripture.
In the beginning was the Word,
and the Word was with God, and the Word was God.
He was in the beginning with God.
All things came into being through him,
and without him not one thing came into being.
What has come into being in him was life,
and the life was the light of all people.
And the Word became flesh and lived among us, and we have seen his glory,
the glory as of a father's only son, full of grace and truth.
From his fullness we have all received, grace upon grace.
(*John 1:1-4, 14, 16*)

Inscription

This inscription may be made with chalk above the entrance:
20 + C M B + 26

Write the appropriate character (left) while speaking the text (right).

The magi of old, known as
C   Caspar,
M   Melchior, and
B   Balthasar,
followed the star of God's Son who came to dwell among us
20 two thousand
26 and twenty-six years ago.
+   Christ, bless this house,
+   and remain with us throughout the new year.

Prayer of Blessing

O God,
you revealed your Son to all people
by the shining light of a star.
We pray that you bless this home and all who live here
with your gracious presence.
May your love be our inspiration, your wisdom our guide,
your truth our light, and your peace our benediction;
through Christ our Lord. Amen.

Then everyone may walk from room to room, blessing the house with incense or by sprinkling with water, perhaps using a branch from the Christmas tree.

Table prayer for Epiphany

Generous God,
you have made yourself known in Jesus, the light of the world.
As this food and drink give us refreshment,
so strengthen us by your spirit,
that as your baptized sons and daughters
we may share your light with all the world.
Grant this through Christ our Lord.
Amen.

Notes

November 30: Gabby Cudjoe-Wilkes and Andrew Wilkes, *Psalms for Black Lives* (Upper Room, 2022), 21. **December 1:** Austen Hartke, *Transforming* (Westminster John Knox, 2023), 159. **December 2:** Cindy Maddox, *In the Neighborhood of Normal* (Regal House, 2021), 8. **December 3:** Dorcas Cheng-Tozun, *Social Justice for the Sensitive Soul* (Broadleaf, 2023), 24. **December 4:** Kaitlyn Schiess, *The Ballot and the Bible* (Brazos, 2023), 34. **December 5:** Becky Chambers, *A Psalm for the Wild-Built* (Tordotcom, 2021), 99. **December 6:** Callie E. Swanlund, *From Weary to Wholehearted* (Church, 2024), 9. **December 7:** Hal Borland, *Countryman: A Summary of Belief* (Lippincott, 1965). **December 8:** Text: Isaac Watts, 1674–1748, "Joy to the world," ELW 267, st. 4. **December 9:** Thomas Bohache, in *The Queer Bible Commentary*, 2nd ed., ed. Robert E. Goss and Mona West (SCM, 2022), 511. **December 10:** Dorothy C. Bass, *Receiving the Day* (Fortress, 2019), 121. **December 11:** Lenny Duncan, *Dear Church* (Fortress, 2019), 8. **December 12:** Martin Luther's final words, various sources. **December 13:** "Ask an Expert: Why Is Prescribed Fire Important?" Interview with Jennifer Fawcett, extension specialist and prescribed fire work group coordinator in the Department of Forestry and Environmental Resources, North Carolina State University, College of Natural Resources, https://cnr.ncsu.edu/news/2021/11/why-is-prescribed-fire-important/. Luther quote: Luther's Small Catechism (Augsburg Fortress, 2017), 38. **December 14:**

Yolanda Pierce, "The Spirituality of Waiting," *The Christian Century*, August 2024, 37. **December 15:** Text: Benjamin Schmolck, 1672–1737; trans. Catherine Winkworth, 1829–1878, alt.; "Open now thy gates of beauty," ELW 533, st. 1. **December 16:** Wes Moore, *The Other Wes Moore* (Penguin Random House, 2011), 163–164. **December 17:** Rachel Naomi Remen, *My Grandfather's Blessings* (Berkley, 2001), 188–189. **December 18:** Michelle Obama, *The Light We Carry* (Crown, 2022), 101. **December 19:** Text: Charles Wesley, 1707–1788; "Come, thou long-expected Jesus," ELW 254, st. 1. **December 20:** Trisha Elliott, "The Many Faces of Jesus," *Broadview*, April 1, 2014, http://broadview.org/the-many-faces-of-jesus/. **December 21:** Gordon W. Lathrop, *Holy Things* (Fortress, 1993), 216. **December 22:** Walter Brueggemann, *The Prophetic Imagination* (Fortress, 2001), 11. **December 23:** Text: James W. Johnson, 1871–1938; "Lift every voice and sing," ELW 841, st. 2. **December 24:** Rosemary Radford Reuther, *Sexism and God-Talk* (Beacon, 1983), 155. **December 25:** Gustavo Gutiérrez, *A Theology of Liberation* (Orbis, 1973), 69. **December 26:** Robin Wall Kimmerer, *Braiding Sweetgrass* (Milkweed, 2013), 104. **December 27:** Craig A. Satterlee, "Commentary on Luke 2:1-14 [15-20]," accessed at www.workingpreacher.org/commentaries/revised-common-lectionary/christmas-eve-nativity-of-our-lord/commentary-on-luke-21-14-15-20-3. **December 28:** United Nations Convention on the Rights of the Child: The Children's Version, www.unicef.org

/child-rights-convention/convention-text-childrens-version. **December 29:** Amanda Held Opelt, *Keening: Grief Ritual Explained*, YouTube video, https://youtu.be/behSNzLL4q U?si=yi_ufdSYifZOSYQK. **December 30:** Abraham Lincoln, "Address Before the Wisconsin State Agricultural Society," 1859, www.abrahamlincolnonline.org/lincoln/speeches/fair.htm. **December 31:** Thomas Wolfe, *You Can't Go Home Again* (Scribner, 1940), www.hoopladigital.com/ebook/you-cant-go-home-again-thomas-wolfe/12334506. **January 1:** Text: Kō Yūki, 1896–1985; tr. composite; © 1978 *Lutheran Book of Worship*, admin. Augsburg Fortress; "In a lowly manger born," ELW 718, st. 1. **January 2:** Jenny Sung, in *Call to Allyship*, ed. Angela T. !Khabeb (Mouth House, 2023), 37. **January 3:** Text: Henry W. Baker, 1821–1877; "The King of love my shepherd is," ELW 502, st. 1. **January 4:** Alice Walker, *The Color Purple* (Harcourt Brace Jovanovich, 1982). **January 5:** Text: African American spiritual, refrain; John W. Work Jr., 1872–1925, sts., alt.; "Go Tell It on the Mountain," *This Far by Faith* 52, st. 3 and refrain. **January 6:** Sharei Green and Beckah Selnick, *God's Holy Darkness* (Beaming, 2022), 11.